D1029215

The Revolutionary War

VOLUME 3

The Revolutionary War

VOLUME 3

Taking up Arms

James R. Arnold & Roberta Wiener

GROLIER
EDUCATIONAL

**First American edition published in 2002
by Grolier Educational**

© 2002 by Graham Beehag Books

Grolier Educational,
90 Sherman Turnpike,
Danbury, Connecticut 06816

Website address: http://publishing.grolier.com

Library of Congress Cataloging-in-Publication Data

The Revolutionary War.
   p. cm.
  Contents: v. 1. The road to rebellion—v. 2. The shot heard around the world—v. 3. Taking up arms—v. 4. The spirit of 1776—v. 5. 1777: a year of decision—v. 6. the road to Valley Forge—v. 7. War of attrition—v. 8. The American cause in peril—v. 9. The turn of the tide —v. 10. An independent nation.
   Includes bibliographical references and indexes.
   ISBN 0-7172-5553-0 (set)—ISBN 0-7172-5554-9 (v. 1)—
ISBN 0-7172-5555-7 (v. 2)—ISBN 0-7172-5556-5 (v. 3)—
ISBN 0-7172-5557-3 (v. 4)—ISBN 0-7172-5558-1 (v. 5)—
ISBN 0-7172-5559-X (v. 6)—ISBN 0-7172-5560-3 (v. 7)—
ISBN 0-7172-5561-1 (v. 8)—ISBN 0-7172-5562-X (v. 9)—
ISBN 0-7172-5563-8 (v. 10)
   1. United States—History—Revolution, 1775–1783—Juvenile literature. [1. united States—History—Revolution. 1775–1783.]
I. Grolier Incorporated.

E208 .R.47 2002
973.3—dc21   2001018998

Printed and bound in Singapore

CONTENTS

CHAPTER ONE

Decisions in London

The Battle of Bunker Hill, June 17, 1775, ended any chance of peace between King George III and his American subjects. Prime Minister North spoke for the king when he said that now the British government was determined to crush the rebellion by force. That meant there would be a war.

North also told the king that there had to be some man in his cabinet to run the war. In the British government the cabinet was a group of top-level leaders. Their job was to manage the nation's business. North knew that he himself was unfit for the job of managing the war. With the king's permission North moved Lord George Germain into the cabinet. For the rest of the war Lord Germain held the key position as **Secretary of State** for the American Colonies.

The 59-year-old Germain had some talents and many flaws. He had military experience. He had served as a general in the Seven Years' War. At an important battle he made a mistake. Germain thought he had done nothing wrong. He demanded a court martial, or official military investigation. The court declared Germain "unfit to serve His Majesty in any military capacity." That decision drove Germain out of the army. So, Germain turned to politics. He proved a good politician. He worked hard and had a great deal of energy. He got on well with King George III.

On the other hand, the position of Secretary of State for the American Colonies put Germain in charge of the military in America. British generals did not like this.

They did not like taking orders from a man who had been disgraced and driven from the army. Generals and politicians need to cooperate to run a war efficiently. Because they did not like Germain, the generals made cooperation difficult.

Germain was also ruthless and petty. He remembered who had helped him and who had been against him. This would lead to many quarrels with important generals during the war. Most important, Germain tried to run the war from London. He and his advisers made

The bloody Battle of Bunker Hill showed the world that there would be a war between the American rebels and the British king. It also taught British generals to be cautious in battle.

the strategy, or the plans for how to fight the war. Then they gave the generals detailed orders telling them what to do. It took time for those orders to cross the Atlantic to America. Often by the time the orders arrived, the situation had changed. It would have been better if Germain had let the generals make their own strategy.

Germain's flaws would become clear as the war went on. In December 1775, when he became Secretary of State for the American Colonies, his flaws were not clear. Germain gave the cabinet a new energy. He began sending regiment after regiment across the Atlantic to reinforce the British army. The king and the cabinet expected that these reinforcements would win the war.

British Opposition to the War

Some British leaders disagreed. They did not think that Britain should make war on America. Since these men were against (or opposed) the government's policy, they were called the opposition. Edmund Burke, Charles Fox, and Charles Rockingham were the key members of the opposition.

Both Burke and Fox were members of the House of Commons. Burke was a great speaker and a clear

Lord North, Lord Germain, John Wilkes, Edmund Burke. Wilkes spoke in favor of the "rights of Englishmen." Burke used "the plain language of truth." Both men opposed the government's policy against the American rebels. Still, the king and Lord North resolved to force the rebels to a "proper constitutional state of obedience."

thinker. He tried to use what he called "the plain language of truth." The American rebels called Burke a friend. Fox was also a fine speaker. People who heard him called his abilities "amazing." Rockingham was a former prime minister. He led the opposition in the House of Lords.

Before fighting began, all three had opposed the anti-American actions of the government. After Bunker Hill they made an effort to keep the peace. Burke proposed a bill in the House of Commons that would calm both sides. Rockingham led nineteen members of the House of Lords to sign a petition against the war. Their efforts failed. It was difficult to oppose the king during times of war.

In 1775 the position of king of England was powerful. But a king needed support from Parliament, with its House of Commons and House of Lords, in order to rule. King George III had firm control over one-third of the members of both houses. That group was called the "King's Friends." The "King's Friends" gave North's government a base of support. North's political task was to build on that base. It proved easy for North and the king to do. They were in a position to give favors to politicians who helped them. By giving favors and making deals, North's government and the king built a solid majority of support in Parliament. So, they were able to ignore the opposition and defeat the efforts of Burke, Fox, and Rockingham.

The fact that most Englishmen were against the American rebels helped North and the king. Englishmen knew that they had paid a big tax to support the army in America during the French and Indian War. They did not understand why the Americans complained about paying a tax that was much smaller. When the ungrateful rebels opened fire against British soldiers at Lexington and Concord, and then fought them again at Bunker Hill, their dislike of the Americans increased enormously.

In summary, the opposition in Parliament was too small and too weak to influence the king and the government. A majority of Englishmen believed that the rebels deserved to be crushed. Last, and most importantly, the king sincerely believed that it was his right and his duty to fight the rebels.

Among the British units sent to America were Scottish Highlanders belonging to the famous Black Watch Regiment.

CHAPTER TWO

Decisions in America

*The Battle of Bunker Hill forced leaders on both sides
to make important decisions.*

Before the battle the British generals—Thomas Gage, John Burgoyne, Henry Clinton, and William Howe —had agreed that they needed to attack the rebels. They

The center of Boston with its Old State House.

had disagreed about how to do it. After the battle they agreed that the army had to leave Boston. Again they disagreed about when and where it should go. Burgoyne wanted to march into Rhode Island. Clinton wanted to march into both Rhode Island and New York. Gage and Howe wanted to sail to Halifax, Nova Scotia, and wait until next spring before continuing the fight. It is difficult to fight a war well when the generals disagree about what to do.

On the rebel side there was no such disagreement. Before the Battle of Bunker Hill the Massachusetts Provincial Congress had asked the Continental Congress to take responsibility for the militia in New England. On June 14, 1775, the Second Continental Congress agreed to do it. That same day it voted to raise ten companies of riflemen from Pennsylvania, Maryland, and Virginia. These riflemen were the first soldiers to be enlisted directly into Continental service. The United States did not yet exist. The regular American military, both army and navy, was called Continental. Soldiers in the Continental Army were called Continentals.

The next day, June 15, Congress appointed George Washington as **commander-in-chief** of the "army of the United Colonies." It was a political decision. The New England colonies had started the Revolution. To win, they needed support from the southern colonies. Virginia was the most powerful southern colony. George Washington was a Virginian.

Washington's military experience was limited. He had spent most of the French and Indian War as a colonel on the Virginia frontier. Commander-in-chief was a huge responsibility. Washington doubted his own ability to do the job. He told fellow Virginian Patrick Henry, "Remember, Mr. Henry, what I now tell you: From the day I

commander-in-chief: the person having the highest authority over a military force

American rifleman (left) and Pennsylvania infantryman. On June 14, 1775, Congress raised its first unit of Continental soldiers. They were riflemen from Pennsylvania, Maryland, and Virginia. Today the U.S. Army accepts June 14, 1775, as its birthday.

11

enter upon the command of the American armies, I date my fall, and the ruin of my reputation."

Still, Washington had some experience that would be useful for commanding the army. His life at Mount Vernon, his Virginia plantation, required him to keep business records, to make decisions about how to spend scarce money, and to plan for both the short run—the next harvest season—and the long term. These skills would be needed for the job of running the army. Also, Washington had political skills. He had served in the Virginia House of Burgesses, the colonial Virginia legislature, and had learned how politicians thought and worked. This was vital knowledge. In the coming years Washington would use his knowledge to work with the members of the Continental Congress.

Congress also appointed four major-generals and eight brigadier-generals to serve under Washington. Because at that time most of the militia were New Englanders, nine of the generals were from New England. Congress chose the other three—Charles Lee, Horatio Gates, and Richard Montgomery—because they had once been

George Washington takes command of the Continental Army at Cambridge, Massachusetts, July 3, 1775.

soldiers in the British army. Congress thought that their experience would help the generals know how to fight and beat the British.

Washington left Philadelphia on June 17, 1775. The Battle of Bunker Hill took place while he was traveling to Boston. He arrived at Cambridge, just outside of Boston, to take command of the army on July 2. The army numbered about 15,000 men. Washington found the army a mix of people "under very little discipline, order or government." Washington would learn that all American militia were like that. They were men who were used to being their own bosses, used to making their own decisions. They did not like having other men tell them what to do.

The Beginning of a Professional Army

Washington began the task of turning the American militia into a professional army. He created badges of rank so that there would be a command structure. From top to bottom: general, colonel, major, captain, lieutenant, ensign, sergeant, corporal, private. Generals cannot do everything by themselves. They need helpers,

Recruits for the first unit of Continental Marines in December 1775.

An American general and his aides.

special officers called staff officers. Staff officers had many important duties. They had to make sure the soldiers had enough of everything—shelter, food, ammunition—to live and fight. They also had to make sure that the commanding general's orders were understood and carried out.

Modern armies use staff officers who attend special schools. The British army in the Revolutionary War used staff officers who had a great deal of experience. George Washington and other rebel generals had to use inexperienced staff officers. Often the staff officers belonged to a general's family or were family friends. Sometimes they were volunteers from important political families.

Some were foreigners who came to America because they wanted to help the Americans. Some were foreigners who were simply looking for jobs. Often, the staff officers were simply smart and eager young men.

Some of these staff officers would learn to do their jobs quite well. Still, because they were not professional military men, they would make many mistakes. Until they learned their jobs, bad staff work prevented the rebel army from working smoothly.

Washington made Horatio Gates, the only other general from Virginia, and one of his few experienced officers, his adjutant-general. That meant that Gates was responsible for preparing regulations and orders. Washington believed that "Discipline is the soul of an army. It makes small numbers formidable." Washington and Gates insisted that the soldiers learn discipline. They could not just leave camp when they felt like it. So, a system of regular roll calls began. If a soldier was not present when the roll was called, other soldiers searched for him. If they found him, he was punished. Punishments included some very severe things such as whippings and the pillory, or stocks.

Washington divided his forces into three groups, with each group commanded by a major-general. Massachusetts General Artemas Ward commanded the right wing, which was the largest group. It was in Roxbury and guarded the overland exit from Boston. General Israel Putnam of Connecticut commanded the center with his headquarters at Cambridge. General Charles Lee, a former officer in the British army, commanded the left. His job was to guard the road leading out of Charlestown.

Inside Boston was a British garrison of about 6,500 men. Both the British and the Americans built fortifications to protect themselves against attack. Soldiers called that kind of situation, where one side surrounded the other but did not attack right away, a siege. History would later describe the campaign as the Siege of Boston. At the time, neither side thought it a good idea to risk an attack. Instead, during the late summer of 1775 both sides made some small raids, but the raids did not accomplish very much. So, both sides sat, watched, and waited.

General Horatio Gates served as Washington's adjutant-general during the Siege of Boston. Later in the war Gates held many important commands.

CHAPTER THREE

Army Organization

Three basic types of soldiers fought the Revolutionary War on land: infantry, men who fought on foot; cavalry, men who rode horses into battle; and artillery, men who worked the big guns. Each type was important, but infantry was the most important of all.

In 1775 the American, or rebel, soldiers were not yet well organized. They were not professional soldiers. Instead, they were militia, citizen-soldiers who had assembled to defend their homes and neighborhoods against British attack. They joined, or enlisted, for either a six-month term or until the end of the year. Their officers formed the individuals into temporary units, but these organizations were not all alike. The smallest, basic unit was a company, which at that time numbered anywhere from 20 to 100 men. A captain commanded a company.

The next basic unit was a regiment. In 1775, because there was not yet a formal organization for the entire army, one group might call themselves a regiment and number 100 men; another regiment might have 300 men. A colonel commanded a regiment. A group of regiments made up a brigade. A junior general, called a brigadier-general, commanded a brigade. A group of brigades formed a division. Senior generals, often with the rank of major-general, commanded a division.

Infantry
For the whole war almost all infantrymen fought with muskets. Unlike modern weapons, they were smoothbore

guns. They fired a lead ball that traveled about 300 yards. But a soldier could fire accurately to a distance of only about 80 yards. A really well-trained soldier might be able to fire a musket once every fifteen seconds.

A few soldiers carried rifles. Rifles had grooves inside their barrels that made the bullet spin. A spinning bullet was much more accurate. An experienced shooter could hit his target at a range of up to 300 yards. However, it took much longer to reload a rifle than a musket.

During the early part of the war only a few Continental regiments received uniforms as good as the uniforms shown here.

American riflemen wore loose fitting "hunting smocks," often made from undyed (uncolored) material.

defenses: a line of fieldworks and forts around an area that an army is defending

The longer weapon is an American rifle. Below it is an American musket. Both weapons were used in the Revolutionary War.

The war's most famous group of riflemen began their service during the Siege of Boston. Captain Daniel Morgan brought a 96-man company of Virginia riflemen to Boston in the summer of 1775. Morgan's riflemen were all experienced hunters. They quickly showed their skill by shooting down British guards who were manning the Boston **defenses**.

Infantry fought in shoulder-to-shoulder formation. A 22-inch gap separated one man from another, just enough

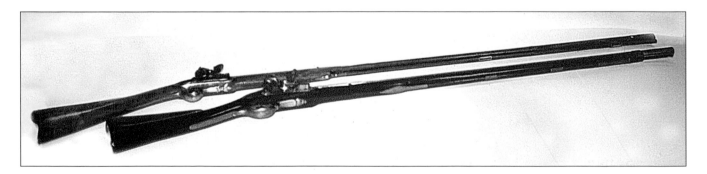

space to let a man load his weapon without bumping into the man next to him. The military idea behind this shoulder-to-shoulder formation was to pack as many muskets into as small a space as possible. That way, when a company all fired at the same time, the shooters had a good chance of hitting a fair number of enemy soldiers. In order to have the best chance of hitting the target, well-trained soldiers waited until the enemy came very near. Then they fired and charged with the bayonet, a type of sword attached to the end of the musket.

It took calm courage to wait for an enemy to move to within 50 or even 20 yards before firing. Professional soldiers trained, or drilled, for months to learn that type of courage. Military men called that ability discipline. During the war's early years the British regular, or professional, soldiers had that kind of discipline. It took time for the rebels to learn discipline. (See the section "How Soldiers Fought" in Volume 2 to learn more.)

At the time of the Revolutionary War European soldiers marched and fought in neat formations. Soldiers stood shoulder to shoulder and were expected to follow orders quickly and without asking questions.

Cavalry

Soldiers who rode horses instead of marching on foot were called cavalrymen. Like the infantry, cavalry also organized into companies and regiments. The main job of the cavalry was to act as fast-moving scouts. They rode ahead and on either side of the infantry and searched for the enemy. During a battle cavalry usually took a position on either side, or flank, of the infantry or stayed behind the infantry (a position called in reserve). They were too valuable to be wasted in the middle of a fight. Instead, they waited for a special opportunity before charging enemy infantry or artillery.

Captain Samuel Morris's 1st Troop of Philadelphia City Cavalry.

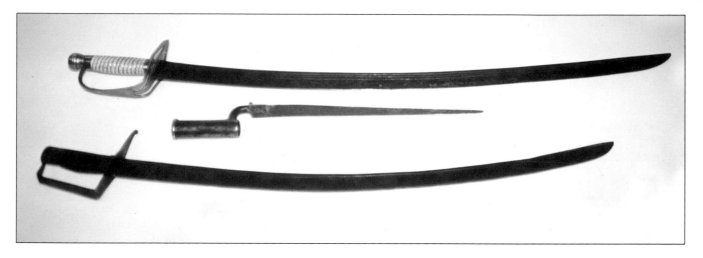

Cavalrymen carried edged weapons, either straight swords or curved **sabers**. Cavalrymen often fought hand to hand. They used their swords and sabers to thrust or hack at the enemy. Cavalrymen also carried pistols and special kinds of light muskets called carbines. They could not fire those weapons very accurately while riding their horses. Once they fired, they could not reload until the fighting ended. Most often, cavalrymen dismounted from their horses in order to use firearms.

Neither the British nor the Americans used a large number of cavalry during the war. There were several reasons. First, cavalrymen need open ground to fight well. They could not stay in formation if there were many obstacles such as woods, fences, or swamps. Most

Edged weapons of the Revolutionary War: saber for cavalry; bayonet for infantry; a short sword called a "hanger" for infantry officers.

saber: a heavy, curved sword carried by cavalrymen. The curve makes it easier for them to strike downward while on horseback.

Well-equipped cavalry usually carried one or two pistols. Pistols were not very accurate and were difficult for a man to aim while riding a horse.

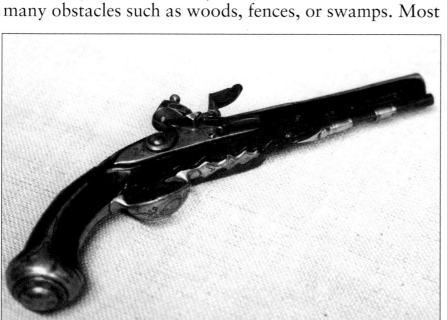

of North America during the years of the Revolutionary War did not have the kind of open ground cavalry needed. Also, horses need to eat quite often. Their food—grain and roughage such as hay and grass—had to be hauled in wagons. The wagons slowed an army down. Because the thirteen colonies were not thickly populated, it was very hard for cavalrymen to find the grain and hay they needed. Last, cavalry forces are much more expensive than foot soldiers. The horses and all of their special equipment like saddles and bridles cost money. The American side did not have even enough money to pay its soldiers, let alone enough to pay to form cavalry units. The British side also had money problems and did not want to spend on cavalry.

Artillery

The artillery of the Revolutionary War was all smoothbore, muzzle-loading weapons. Cannons fired solid, iron balls (called solid shot) straight ahead out of their muzzles. The balls struck the target with great force, knocking men down like pins in a bowling alley. Howitzers lobbed hollow, iron shells filled with gunpowder high into the air. A lit fuse caused the shell to explode. Metal fragments would then scatter and hit nearby targets.

Cannons were defined by the weight of the shot they fired. A 3-pounder gun fired a three-pound solid shot. A bigger gun such as a 12-pounder fired a twelve-pound shot. Howitzers were defined by the size of their opening or muzzle. An 8-inch howitzer had an eight-inch muzzle.

The smaller, lighter guns used in battle were usually 3-, 4-, 6-, or 12-pounder weapons. They were called field pieces because they were used in the field. They fired accurately up to 900 yards. Their maximum range was much more. A solid shot that missed its target would roll and bounce for hundreds of yards. It was still dangerous while it rolled. Cannons fired solid shot

against formed groups of men or against light buildings. The solid shot were not effective against well-built earthworks.

For close-range fighting against infantry and cavalry, both guns and howitzers fired canister. Canister was a tin container holding small iron balls. After leaving the muzzle, the container broke apart to scatter the iron balls in a deadly pattern. In that way a canister shot was like a giant shotgun blast. Good gun crews could fire two rounds a minute from the lighter guns and one round a minute from the heavier 12-pounders.

Artillery was made from bronze or iron. The guns were heavy. The lightest 3-pounder weighed 500 pounds. The 12-pounder weighed almost one ton. Teams of horses or oxen pulled the guns along the roads during a march. The drivers were civilians. When the battle started, the civilians moved to the rear. On the battlefield the cannoneers, the men who worked the guns, hauled on drag ropes to move the guns into position.

The great weight of the bigger guns prevented them from being moved easily. So the biggest guns were kept at forts. Big guns, or heavy artillery, were needed to attack fortifications, including forts or earthworks. Such guns were called siege guns. They would be moved into position with great difficulty and then used to knock a hole in a fort's wall or to knock apart earthworks.

The rebel army outside of Boston needed some big siege guns in order to drive the British from the port. When Ethan Allen captured Fort Ticonderoga on May 10, 1775, he found the fort full of heavy artillery. But Fort Ticonderoga was 300 miles from Boston. There were no good roads connecting the fort with Boston. It seemed that all that good artillery was useless to Washington and his army. A young officer named Henry Knox was thinking about the problem. In November he would go to Washington's headquarters to propose a solution. Meanwhile, there was another campaign taking place north of Fort Ticonderoga. American forces were invading Canada!

An American gun crew in action. Each field gun had a basic crew of five gunners to load, aim, and fire the gun.

CHAPTER FOUR

The Invasion of Canada

Fifteen years before the Revolutionary War Canada had been controlled by France. During the French and Indian War (1754-1763) Canada had served as a base for the French and their Indian allies to attack southward into the American colonies.

When England won the war, it made Canada a British province. By 1775 most Canadians still spoke French and had more loyalty to France than to England. American rebel leaders thought that they could take advantage of the situation. Some patriot groups looked hopefully toward Canada and thought that it might join the Revolution as a fourteenth colony.

So, Congress sent messengers to Canada to learn if the Canadians wanted to join the rebellion. They found that a wise British governor, General Guy Carleton, had healed most of the differences from the last war. The Canadians were perfectly happy to stay in the British empire. But Congressional strategists feared that the British might use Canada in the same way that the French had used it, namely, as a base to attack southward. To prevent it, Congress planned an invasion of Canada.

The American invasion of 1775 had two parts. One part was to push north from Ticonderoga toward Montreal. Philip Schuyler commanded that effort.

Before the Revolutionary War British colonists fought French colonists in several wars. Back in 1745 Massachusetts soldiers had captured the French fortress at Louisbourg as shown here. The history of fighting between Americans and Canadians meant that Canadians were not too likely to want to help the American rebels.

24

However, soon after the advance began, Schuyler fell sick. Thus his chief lieutenant, General Richard Montgomery, actually commanded the invasion. Montgomery's entire force numbered about 3,000 Massachusetts, Connecticut, and New York soldiers.

Left: General Richard Montgomery was a former British officer. He married into a strong rebel family and became a devoted American patriot.

A Connecticut patriot named Benedict Arnold led the second part of the invasion. Arnold was a very ambitious man. He had tried to get an important position under Schuyler. When that failed, Arnold thought up a plan to invade Canada by using a different route. Arnold's plan called for a force to follow the Kennebec River through Maine and enter Canada by the Chaudière River. This river led to the most important city in Canada, Quebec.

George Washington liked the idea. He thought that Arnold's effort would attract British attention away from Schuyler. Since Washington approved of Arnold's plan, Congress decided to let Arnold go ahead. Arnold recruited about 1,200 men from Pennsylvania, Maryland, and Virginia. Among them were the Virginia riflemen commanded by Daniel Morgan.

On August 30, 1775, Montgomery led an advance guard on the first leg of the journey to Montreal. Twelve days later Arnold left Cambridge, Massachusetts, on the first leg of his march to Quebec. There were several problems with the American strategy. Many miles of wilderness separated Montgomery's and Arnold's forces. That made it impossible for them to work together. The Americans believed that once they arrived in Canada, they would be welcomed by the Canadians. That turned out not to be true. Last, Arnold's planned route followed an Indian trail that was so rugged even the Indians had seldom used it. Whether an army could use such a route was unknown.

Left: Benedict Arnold was short, stout, and red-faced. He was brave to the point of rashness and refused to accept that anything was impossible. His energy, drive, and courage inspired his soldiers.

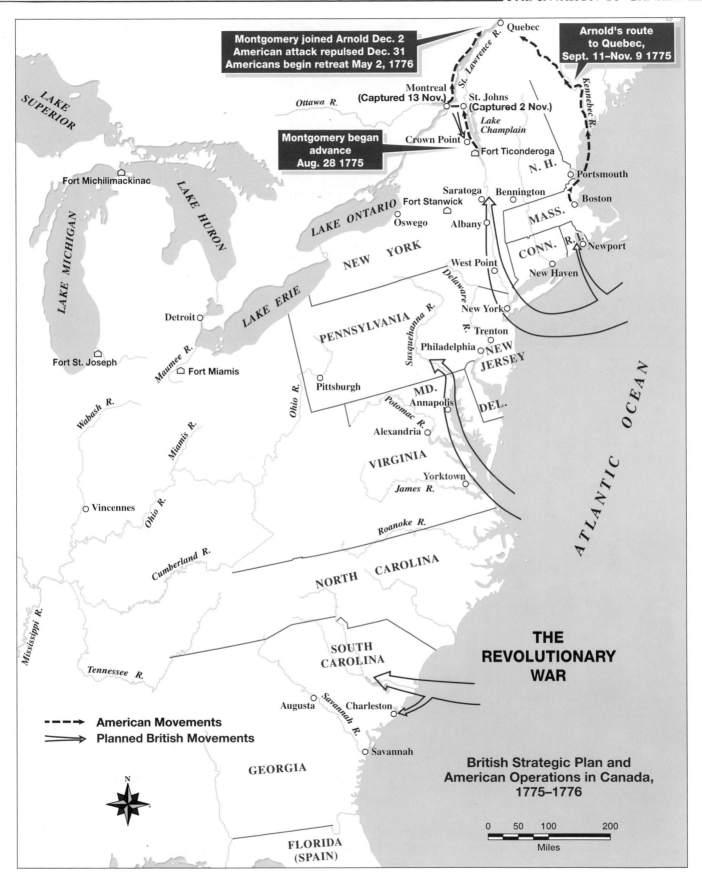

Montgomery joined Arnold Dec. 2
American attack repulsed Dec. 31
Americans begin retreat May 2, 1776

Arnold's route
to Quebec,
Sept. 11–Nov. 9 1775

Quebec

St. Lawrence R.

Ottawa R.

Montreal
(Captured 13 Nov.)

St. Johns
(Captured 2 Nov.)

Kennebec R.

Lake Champlain

Montgomery began
advance
Aug. 28 1775

Crown Point

Fort Ticonderoga

N. H.

Portsmouth

LAKE SUPERIOR

Fort Michilimackinac

LAKE MICHIGAN

LAKE HURON

Saratoga

Bennington

Boston

Fort Stanwick

MASS.

LAKE ONTARIO

Oswego

Albany

CONN.

R. I.

Newport

NEW YORK

West Point

New Haven

Detroit

LAKE ERIE

Delaware R.

Susquehanna R.

New York

Fort St. Joseph

Maumee R.

Fort Miamis

PENNSYLVANIA

Trenton

R.

Philadelphia

NEW JERSEY

Ohio R.

Pittsburgh

MD.

Annapolis

DEL.

Wabash R.

Miamis R.

Potomac R.

Alexandria

VIRGINIA

Vincennes

Ohio R.

Yorktown

James R.

ATLANTIC OCEAN

Roanoke R.

Cumberland R.

NORTH CAROLINA

Mississippi R.

THE
REVOLUTIONARY
WAR

SOUTH
CAROLINA

Tennessee R.

Augusta

Savannah R.

Charleston

- - - ➤ American Movements
——➤ Planned British Movements

N

Savannah

GEORGIA

British Strategic Plan and
American Operations in Canada,
1775–1776

0   50   100   200
Miles

FLORIDA
(SPAIN)

Between Lake Champlain and the St. Lawrence River was a small fort at St. Johns. The British commander in Canada, Governor Guy Carleton, sent a force of 662 men to defend the fort. Montgomery arrived at St. Johns on September 5, 1775. He decided to lay siege to the fort. Then, unexpectedly, Ethan Allen showed up.

After his capture of Fort Ticonderoga Allen had quarreled with his cousin, Seth Warner, over the leadership of the Green Mountain Boys. Since that time

The defeat and capture of Ethan Allen near Montreal on September 25, 1775.

skirmish: a brief battle involving a small number of soldiers; often part of a larger battle

Allen had been without a command. He showed up at Montgomery's headquarters to offer his services. Montgomery was eager to get rid of Allen. He sent him ahead to try to recruit Canadians for the American cause.

Instead, Allen persuaded another officer to join him in an attempt to capture Montreal. Allen hoped to recreate his feat at Fort Ticonderoga by capturing Montreal before that city was on guard. But the British learned about Allen's approach. A small British force, most of whom were French Canadian and English militia, attacked Allen and his men on September 25, 1775. The result was a total defeat for the Americans. The British even captured Allen himself.

Before the **skirmish** many Canadians doubted that Canada could defend itself from the Americans. They wondered if they should help the Americans or at least stay out of the fight. When people saw the fearsome figure of Ethan Allen being put aboard a ship to take him to London, where he would stand trial for treason to King George, most people changed their minds. They decided to support the British and resist the Americans.

On November 2, 1775, St. Johns finally surrendered. The siege had lasted 55 days. The gallant British resistance had badly delayed Montgomery's advance. Still, Montgomery was a very determined leader. He continued on to Montreal. The British evacuated the city, and the Americans marched in on November 13. The first snows had already fallen. Despite the fact that winter was fast approaching, Montgomery decided to go ahead and try to capture Quebec at the end of November. However, most of his men had enlisted for only a short time. Also, they were not dressed for a

The Siege of St. Johns delayed the American invasion of Canada for 55 days.

Arnold's men had to carry their boats around the most dangerous rapids. Sometimes they had to carry their boats for several miles to get past a single stretch of rapids.

winter campaign. Having captured Montreal, they saw no reason to continue and face both the British and a harsh Canadian winter. Montgomery managed to persuade only about 300 men to join him for the march to Quebec.

During the time Montgomery was moving on Montreal, Benedict Arnold was leading his men through the Maine wilderness. At that time few people lived in

Maine. Maine was not even a colony, but instead was part of Massachusetts. The march through Maine was terribly difficult. The soldiers moved by boat along the Kennebec River. They came to a dangerous set of rapids where many of their boats were wrecked and their supplies soaked. It took three days to pass this obstacle. The column carried on, but now they traveled through an empty region where no humans lived and where there were no fresh supplies. The soaking caused the supplies that they carried with them to spoil.

The men became desperately hungry. They killed an officer's dog and ate it. They washed their moosehide moccasins and boiled them for food. One dinner was the jawbone of a pig boiled in water to make a thin soup. Some soldiers voted to turn back. Only Arnold's great energy and spirit kept most of the soldiers moving ahead.

Arnold reached the St. Lawrence River, opposite Quebec, on November 9. His force had shrunk to only about 700 hungry men. On December 2 Montgomery joined him. Inside of Quebec the well-fed and warm British garrison numbered about 1,126 men. They knew

On one stretch of river, called the Dead River, Arnold's men had to row about thirty miles against the current.

31

Arnold's surviving troops assembling just across the river from Quebec.

that time was on their side. If they could hold out until spring, reinforcements were sure to come sailing up the St. Lawrence River. Outside the walls the Americans knew that time was not on their side. The army grew smaller as men deserted or became sick. The terms of enlistment for many soldiers ended when the new year came. Montgomery and Arnold knew that if they were to succeed, they had to strike before the end of December.

The two generals decided that their best chance was to

Arnold's division attacking Quebec through the snow on the night of December 31.

attack during a snowstorm and while it was still dark. They made plans to attack Quebec from two different directions. They hoped to surprise the British inside the city. However, American deserters alerted the garrison that the Americans would attack soon. So, when the attack came in the early morning hours of December 31, it was no surprise.

The brave Montgomery led his men forward through a howling blizzard. Suddenly a group of unseen defenders opened fire. Montgomery fell dead. Most of the

American soldiers in the leading group were hit. Only a few—including Captain Aaron Burr, a future U.S. vice-president—were unhurt. A New York colonel took command. He was not up to the difficult job. He ordered a retreat.

Meanwhile, the brave Arnold had led his column against another part of Quebec. There too the defenders spotted the Americans. They opened a heavy fire. Arnold received a serious wound. The commander of the Virginia riflemen, Daniel Morgan, tried to carry on. He crossed the first barrier only to be blasted from the top of a scaling ladder (a ladder used to climb over the wall of a fort) and knocked down into the snow.

Above: The death of Montgomery beneath the walls of Quebec.

Opposite top: Daniel Morgan had to surrender to the defenders of Quebec.

Opposite below: British troops meeting Daniel Morgan's men as they climb over the city walls to attack Quebec.

Morgan got up and led his men forward again. They struck a well-defended wall and could go no further. The British circled around behind them and forced Morgan and a number of his men to surrender.

The attack had been an American disaster; Montgomery killed, Arnold wounded, Morgan captured. In total the Americans lost about 460 men, including 389 who were captured. The British lost fewer than 20 men. For a while Arnold kept the army outside of Quebec. But it was too weak to take the city. Some reinforcements came, but more Americans fell sick. Smallpox and other diseases killed many soldiers. Everyone knew that when spring came, the Americans would have to retreat to save themselves.

CHAPTER FIVE

The Siege of Boston

The autumn of 1775 brought little change in Boston.

In September a Congressional committee visited Washington's army. They helped make a plan to create a new army. It would be enlisted directly into Continental service; in other words, it would be a national army. There would be 26 infantry regiments of 728 men each as well as one regiment of riflemen and one of artillery. The total force of 20,372 would be paid and supplied by the Continental Congress. Soldiers were to enlist for one year.

It was a good plan, except for having the soldiers enlist for only one year. It proved easier to make a plan on paper than to make a new army. The men who were serving in the army outside of Boston believed that they had done enough. Their families and their farms needed them. They did not want to enlist for another year. Also, officers and men did not much like the idea of serving in the Continental Army. They were used to being in militia units formed of their neighbors and friends. They did not like the idea of serving with strangers.

On December 10, 1775, most of the Connecticut militia went home. Three weeks later the terms of enlistment for thousands of other militia ended, and those soldiers went home also. The strength of the army declined to about 8,000 men. Washington complained that he would be happier serving as a private rather than trying to command a force that could hardly be called an army.

On the British side there was one important change. The Secretary of State for the American Colonies, Lord

Richard Montgomery

Richard Montgomery was born in Ireland in 1738. After attending college, he joined the British army when he was 18 and fought in Canada and the Caribbean. He returned to England, where he had many friends, but decided in 1772 to resign from the army, move to New York, and take up farming. In 1775 Montgomery joined the Continental Army with the rank of brigadier-general. As a newlywed, he did this out of duty rather than enthusiasm for army life. After his death in battle at Quebec only a few months later both British and American people praised him highly. They contrasted his courage in marching to Quebec with the inaction of the British commander comfortably holed up in Boston.

Germain, had decided that General Thomas Gage was not the man to command the British army in America. Germain did not think that Gage was aggressive and ruthless enough. On September 26, 1775, Gage received orders to return home. Gage arrived back in London on November 14. British officials treated him poorly. They took away most of his pay and privileges and forced him to retire.

General William Howe replaced Gage. Howe had won a reputation as a smart and inventive officer. He had helped develop the British light infantry. They were elite troops who used modern tactics. General Howe was also good at training and supplying his troops. At the Battle of Bunker Hill Howe had shown great bravery. Howe decided that his best strategy was to keep the British army in Boston until the spring of 1776.

"The Noble Train of Artillery"

Nothing would have changed at the Siege of Boston except that a 25-year-old man named Henry Knox had an idea. Knox had joined the militia at age 18. He had seen the Boston Massacre and had tried to stop the British commander from ordering his men to fire into the mob. In 1775 Knox was the owner of a Boston

Big, beefy Henry Knox was a self-taught military man.

bookstore. He had always been interested in military matters and read everything he could find. The subject of the artillery particularly fascinated the big, beefy young man. Because he had lost two fingers in a hunting accident, Knox could not serve as an infantryman. So, he served at the Battle of Bunker Hill as an aide, or helper, to General Ward. He met Washington on July 5, 1775, and impressed the army commander. Washington named Knox the colonel of the newly created Continental Regiment of Artillery in the fall of 1775. It was an important-sounding title with only one problem: The regiment hardly existed.

Knox suggested to Washington that he would go to Fort Ticonderoga and bring back the heavy guns. Even though the fort was 300 miles away, Washington told Knox to go ahead and try. Knox arrived at Fort Ticonderoga on December 5. He selected 50 or 60 of the best cannons and mortars (so named because they look like a pharmacist's mortar, a military mortar is a short

Fort Ticonderoga with its guns overlooking Lake Champlain.

Oxen haul the sledges carrying the heavy guns from Fort Ticonderoga to Boston.

gun that lobs its shot at a high angle into the air; in this way it can fire over walls and buildings). Knox called these weapons his "Noble Train of Artillery." The problem was how to move his train through a New England winter to Boston.

Knox showed great energy and drive. He ordered 42 heavy sleds (called sledges) built. He brought 80 pairs of oxen to the fort to haul the sledges. Men placed the guns

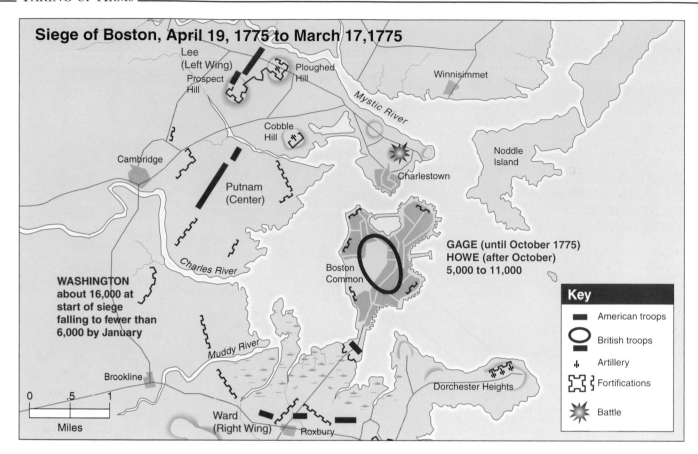

Siege of Boston, April 19, 1775 to March 17, 1775

Lee (Left Wing)
Ploughed Hill
Prospect Hill
Winnisimmet
Mystic River
Cobble Hill
Noddle Island
Cambridge
Charlestown
Putnam (Center)
GAGE (until October 1775)
HOWE (after October)
5,000 to 11,000
Charles River
Boston Common
WASHINGTON
about 16,000 at
start of siege
falling to fewer than
6,000 by January
Muddy River
Brookline
0 .5 1
Miles
Dorchester Heights
Ward (Right Wing)
Roxbury

Key
■ American troops
⬭ British troops
⫟ Artillery
❖ Fortifications
✸ Battle

on the sledges, and off through the snows the train moved. The total weight of the guns and mortars was 119,900 pounds. Three of the giant mortars weighed one ton each. Progress was slow at times. The column moved past Fort Edward, Saratoga, and Albany, New York, and on to Springfield, Massachusetts. There were steep mountains to cross. It snowed heavily in the Berkshire Mountains. Still, to everyone's surprise, Knox succeeded. His "Noble Train" arrived outside of Boston before the end of January 1776.

Until the guns arrived, the rebel army was in a bad way. Neither Congress, the colonies, nor Washington had worked out who was responsible for what. When no one took charge, the system broke down. This was to happen time and time again during the war. Although Congress had ordered an army of 20,370 men, there were only 8,212 men enlisted on January 14, 1776. Only 5,582 of them were present and fit for duty. The soldiers were poorly clothed and poorly fed. Many sickened and died.

Washington believed that even that small number would soon become fewer. He also knew that the British would get reinforcements. Washington held a meeting of his generals. Such a military meeting is called a council of war. Washington convinced his generals that the army had to attack Boston before the spring. Since he did not have enough Continental soldiers to make the attack, he called for more militia to join his army. On February 16 Washington suggested to his generals that the army take advantage of the cold weather that had frozen the water of part of Boston Harbor. Washington proposed a surprise attack across the ice. Fortunately, his generals opposed this risky plan.

It was at that point that Knox's artillery became important. Bringing the siege guns to Boston was a tremendous accomplishment. The guns gave Washington and his army a way to drive the British from Boston. On March 2, 1776, American guns west of Boston opened fire against the British positions. That bombardment was a feint, or fake, designed to attract British attention.

Knox's "Noble Train of Artillery" arrives outside of Boston.

Meanwhile, Americans spent the night building a fortification on Dorchester Heights, northeast of Boston. Because the ground was frozen, trenches could not be dug. Instead, the rebels filled large baskets with stone and dirt (called gabions) and used them to make an above-ground breastworks. Then they put some of Knox's siege guns behind the gabions.

Howe and his generals spotted the rebel battery on Dorchester Heights the next morning. They immediately saw that the battery was a serious threat since the guns could block movement into and out of the harbor. Howe ordered an attack. A severe storm on the night of March 4 gave Howe an excuse to cancel the attack. Howe was happy for the excuse because he worried that an attack on Dorchester Heights might cause heavy losses. It might be like another Battle of Bunker Hill.

Rebel gunners build a battery on Dorchester Heights while officers study the view of Boston Harbor.

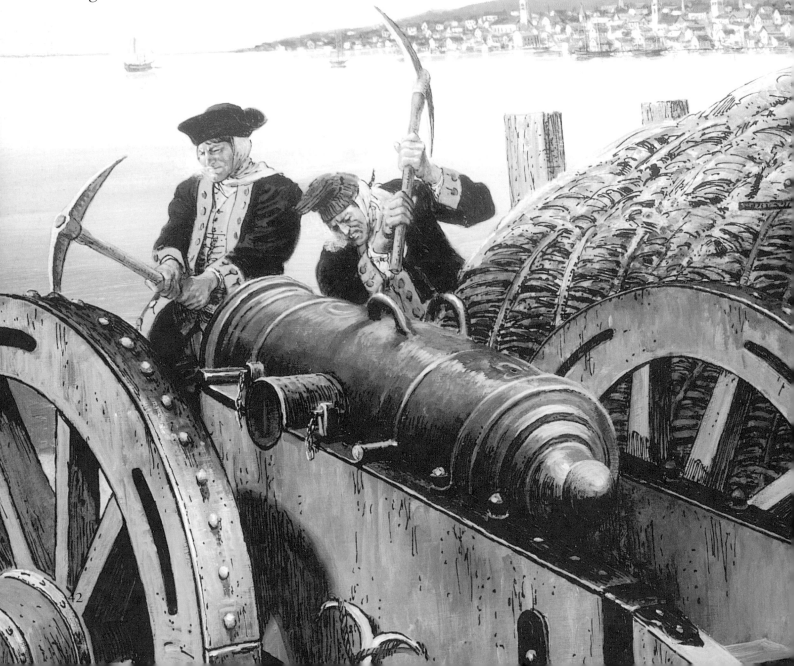

42

Ever since the Battle of Bunker Hill Howe had thought that leaving Boston was the best strategy. Now that the rebels had powerful guns controlling the harbor, on March 7 he gave the order to leave. On March 17 the British evacuated the city. Ships carried away 11,000 British soldiers and sailors as well as nearly 1,000 loyalists. Leaving was particularly hard for the loyalists, or Tories. They left behind their homes and businesses. The ships sailed for Halifax, Nova Scotia.

The Siege of Boston was a great American victory. It had lasted eight months. During that time the Americans lost fewer than 20 men killed in combat. George Washington had held together a rebel army made up mostly of civilian-soldiers against the professional military might of Great Britain, the world's strongest nation. That was an amazing accomplishment.

Because the British did not have enough ships to carry away everything, they left behind valuable military supplies. The rebels found 69 useful cannons, many medical supplies, and 3,000 blankets. British soldiers never returned to Boston. For the rest of the war there was no fighting in Massachusetts, the place where the rebellion had begun.

Howe evacuates Boston on March 17, 1776. The British left behind much valuable equipment, including 69 useful pieces of artillery.

CHAPTER SIX

The Conflict Spreads South

News of the fighting in the north spread through the middle and southern colonies.

The rebellion against King George began in New England. It took time for news about the important events around Boston to spread. Express riders had rapidly carried southward news of the fighting at Lexington and Concord (April 19, 1775). The news reached Charleston, South Carolina, on May 10, 1775. No one was certain what the news meant. Most people in the southern colonies waited and watched. Then came news about the Battle of Bunker Hill. At that point people began to act.

Military action in Virginia began at the coastal port of Norfolk. Norfolk was Virginia's largest town, with 6,000 people. Wealthy citizens knew that rebel leaders, men like Patrick Henry, were meeting in nearby Williamsburg. These citizens worried about what the rebels might do. They called on the royal governor, John Murray, the Earl of Dunmore, and asked for help. Dunmore had only a very few British regulars. Still, he

Left: Patrick Henry was one of the rebels who called for action in Williamsburg. Royal governor Dunmore did not have very much military strength to fight Henry and the other Virginia rebels.

occupied Norfolk with these regulars, some loyal Scottish clerks, and a unit of armed slaves.

American patriots responded by gathering 300 militia from two nearby counties. Dunmore had no fear of militia. He ordered his ragtag force to attack the militia at the town of Kempville. Dunmore's bold plan worked, and his force drove the militia from the field. Their success caused several thousand men to come to Norfolk to swear allegiance to the king.

Patrick Henry

Patrick Henry was born on the Virginia frontier in 1736, just after his family moved there from Scotland. His parents were well educated and taught him at home. When he was 15 years old, he got a job at a country store, and the next year he and his brother opened their own store. Henry got married at the age of 18 and became a farmer. A few years later he lost his home in a fire and had to go back to work as a shopkeeper to support his wife and children. He needed to make more money, so he became a lawyer. His public speaking ability helped him win most of his cases.

Soon, Henry's success as a lawyer led him to the House of Burgesses (the Virginia state government), where he represented the interests of frontier people. In 1775 Henry encouraged people to fight for independence in his most famous speech, in which he said, "Give me liberty, or give me death!" He led a militia force to the state capital to protest against Lord Dunmore's (the royal governor) seizure of an arsenal and made Dunmore back down. Dunmore took revenge by publishing a poster telling people not to help Henry (see illustration). However, the Virginia militia threw Dunmore out of the state, and Patrick Henry was soon elected governor of Virginia in Dunmore's place.

By *the* LION *&* UNICORN, Dieu & mon droit, *their Lieutenant-Generals, Governours, Vice Admirals, &c. &c. &c. &c.*

A HUE & CRY.

WHEREAS I have been informed, from undoubted authority, that a certain PATRICK HENRY, of the county of Hanover, and a number of *deluded followers*, have taken up arms, chofen their officers, and, ftyling themfelves an *independent company*, have marched out of their county, encamped, and put themfelves in a pofture of war; and have written and defpatched letters to divers parts of the country, exciting the people to join in thefe *outrageous* and *rebellious* practices, to the *great terrour* of all his Majefty's *faithful* fubjects, and in *open defiance* of *law* and *government;* and have *committed other acts of violence*, particularly in *extorting* from his *Majefty's Receiver-General* the fum of 330l. under *pretence* of *replacing the powder* I *thought proper* to order from the magazine; whence it undeniably appears, there is *no longer* the leaft fecurity for the *life* or *property* of any man: Wherefore, I have *thought proper, with the advice of his Majefty's Council*, and *in his Majefty's name*, to iffue this *my* proclamation, ftrictly charging *all perfons*, upon their *allegiance*, not to *aid, abet*, or *give countenance* to the faid PATRICK HENRY, or *any other perfons* concerned in *fuch unwarrantable combinations;* but, on the contrary, to oppofe *them*, and *their defigns*, by *every means*, which defigns muft otherwife inevitably involve the *whole country* in the *moft direful calamity*, as they will call for the *vengeance* of *offended Majefty*, and the *infulted laws*, to be *exerted here*, to vindicate the *conftitutional* authority of government.

Given, &c. this 6th day of May, 1775.

D * * * *.

G * * d * * * the P * * * *.

An official British broadside, or poster, attacking Patrick Henry for his efforts to start a revolt.

Dunmore raised two loyalist regiments: the Queen's Own Loyal Virginia Regiment and the Royal Ethiopian Regiment, a unit of black men most of whom were freed slaves. Dunmore sent those regiments on raids along the Virginia coast. The goal was to free slaves and recruit them for Dunmore's growing army.

Colonel William Woodford led a patriot force of 700 Virginia and 200 North Carolina militia against Dunmore's base in Norfolk. Dunmore ordered his 500 men to fortify a position at a place called Great Bridge. The position was at the end of a long causeway, or raised road, that ran through a big tidal swamp. The rebels saw that it was impossible to attack. So they too built a fortification at the other end of the causeway.

One officer serving in Woodford's command was Lieutenant John Marshall. According to legend, a servant who worked for Marshall's father pretended to desert to the British. The servant told the British that the rebels were very weak. Whether that was true or not, for some reason Dunmore ordered an attack over Great Bridge on December 9, 1775.

A force of 60 British grenadiers led the attack. The American defenders drove back the grenadiers. The captain commanding the grenadiers brought up two cannons to help. Then he attacked again. The rebels waited until the British were only 50 yards away. They fooled the British captain into thinking that the Americans had abandoned the fort. He raised his hat to urge his men forward and shouted, "The day is our own." The captain rushed forward only to fall dead from the defenders' fire.

His sudden death discouraged the British. They retreated from the field. The Americans captured the two cannons along with 16 wounded British soldiers. Total British losses were 62 men killed, wounded, and captured. Only one rebel was slightly wounded.

The Battle of Great Bridge was the first fight between British soldiers and American rebels since Bunker Hill. Five days after the battle Woodford led his men into Norfolk. Dunmore and his men crowded aboard ships just offshore. Frustrated and angry, on January 1, 1776, Dunmore ordered the ships to open fire against the town. The bombardment destroyed Norfolk. It was such a brutal action that it ended almost all support for the king in the colony of Virginia for the rest of the war.

North Carolina

The first important military operations in North Carolina took place in January 1776. Like many of the colonies, North Carolina was deeply divided about the rebellion against the king. When patriots heard the news of the fighting in Massachusetts, they became active. They chased the North Carolina royal governor, Josiah Martin, from the capital at New Bern. He arrived at Fort Johnston on the lower Cape Fear River on June 2, 1775. Even there he was not safe. Because the North Carolina militia were fast

According to legend, Lieutenant John Marshall had an important role at the Battle of Great Bridge on December 9, 1775.

Below: A type of fort called a blockhouse used during the American Revolution. Royal governor Martin had to abandon and burn Fort Johnston on the North Carolina coast.

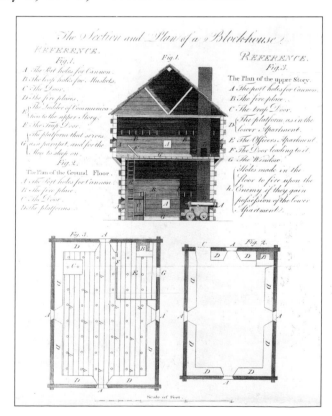

approaching, Martin boarded a British warship and ordered the fort burned.

Martin began planning how to retake North Carolina. He decided to raise an army of 10,000 men. Martin planned to use two special groups to form the army: the Regulators and the Scottish Highlanders. The Regulators were a group of poor people living in the North Carolina hill country. The wealthy merchants and planters living along the coast controlled the colony. Beginning in 1768, the Regulators began protesting that such control was unfair. Protests led to violence. The Regulators fought against the royal governor's men and lost the Battle of Alamance on May 16, 1771. Then they surrendered and swore to stay loyal to the royal governor.

In 1775 Governor Martin believed that he could depend on the loyalty of the Regulators. He thought that the Regulators would make up one-third of his army. The other two-thirds would come from the Scottish Highlanders who lived in western North Carolina. Back in Scotland, they had rebelled against King George II and been defeated in 1746. The defeated Highlanders had pledged to stay loyal to the king. In return, the Crown gave them royal land grants in North Carolina.

Modern-day reenactors show how the Battle of Moore's Creek took place. The Highlanders, including a soldier on the left carrying a shield and broadsword, advance.

The site of the bridge at Moore's Creek.

But the Highlanders had to surrender all of their muskets and pistols so that they could never again fight against the king.

On January 10, 1776, Martin called for all loyal subjects to unite to crush "a most daring horrid, and unnatural Rebellion." Instead of 10,000 men, about 1,300 Scots and 300 other loyalists gathered. They included about 130 Regulators. The Highlanders were armed mostly with their traditional swords and shields. They marched toward the North Carolina coast to join the governor.

A patriot force numbering about 1,000 men gathered to intercept and fight the governor's men. Two patriot officers, Colonel Alexander Lillington and Colonel Richard Caswell, commanded them. Their force took position at Moore's Creek Bridge, about 17 miles from Wilmington, North Carolina. They expected the Highlanders to try to cross the bridge. So, they took up the planks from the middle of the bridge. They spread soft soap and animal fat over the bridge supports to make them slippery. They set up two cannons to shoot at the bridge. The rebel infantry stood behind earthworks in a position where they too could fire at the bridge.

The Highlanders reached Moore's Creek Bridge on February 27, 1776. Eighty of the best swordsmen led the way. The Scottish bagpipes played a war tune. The Highlanders shouted their war cry, "Broadswords and King George!" Then they charged. They did not know that the planks in the middle of the bridge were missing.

The Highlanders tried to walk carefully over the gap, but they slipped on the grease. The defenders' cannons fired canister, and the infantry fired their muskets. The Highlanders had no guns to fire back with. The ambush surprised and discouraged the Highlanders. Rebel fire killed 30 Highlanders, including their two leaders, and wounded 40 more. The North Carolina militia lost only one man killed and one wounded.

The militia did not pursue the defeated Highlanders. Instead, they began to loot the baggage wagons that belonged to the Highlanders. Later, the 1st Regiment of North Carolina Continentals arrived. They did pursue

Missing planks forced the Highlanders to try to scramble across the bridge at Moore's Creek.

the scattered Highlanders. Eventually, they captured about 850 men. Most of the Highlanders signed a parole, a pledge to go home and not fight.

The Battle of Moore's Creek was small but important. About 10,000 Highland Scots lived in North Carolina. The defeat at Moore's Creek discouraged them. They remained loyal to the king. But they did not become active until British troops arrived in the South in 1780. Until then, because of Moore's Creek, the patriot cause was able to control North Carolina.

South Carolina

Late in the fall of 1775 a 70-year-old militia colonel, Richard Richardson, joined up with a famous Indian fighter named William Thomson. Thomson's nickname was "Danger." The two men collected 2,500 militia and marched deep into the South Carolina back country. The goal was to attack a large group of loyalists led by Patrick Cuningham and Colonel Thomas Fletchall.

There were several brief skirmishes, and the rebels won them all. After one combat some of Thomson's men discovered Colonel Fletchall hiding in a hollow tree. They captured the loyalist leader. But the main group of loyalists kept retreating deeper into the wilderness.

More militia reinforced Colonel Richardson until his command numbered about 4,000 men. Richardson learned that Cuningham and a large group of loyalists were camped at a place called Canebrake. Canebrake was over the South Carolina border on Cherokee tribal land. Richardson sent "Danger" Thomson to attack the loyalist camp. Thomson surrounded the camp during the night and charged at dawn on December 22, 1775. A short fight took place, but the rebels quickly won. They killed 6 loyalists and captured 130 more. But Patrick Cuningham jumped onto a horse and rode bareback, without a saddle, to safety.

After the battle Colonel Richardson marched his militia back home. Heavy snow fell, making it a difficult march. Men remembered it forever after as the "Snow Campaign." Richardson's campaign was useful for the American cause. It kept the loyalists in South Carolina from growing strong and active.

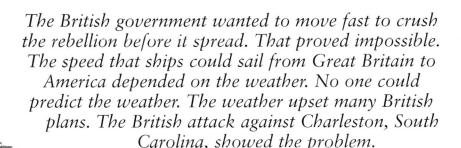

CHAPTER SEVEN

The British Attack Charleston

General Henry Clinton was second in command to General Howe. Clinton was brave. He led the final attack at Bunker Hill. Clinton was full of good advice for Howe, and Howe did not like it. So, Howe got rid of Clinton by sending him to command the Charleston Expedition of 1776.

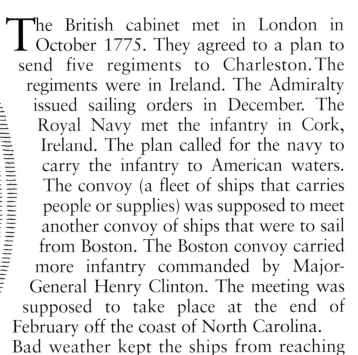

The British government wanted to move fast to crush the rebellion before it spread. That proved impossible. The speed that ships could sail from Great Britain to America depended on the weather. No one could predict the weather. The weather upset many British plans. The British attack against Charleston, South Carolina, showed the problem.

The British cabinet met in London in October 1775. They agreed to a plan to send five regiments to Charleston. The regiments were in Ireland. The Admiralty issued sailing orders in December. The Royal Navy met the infantry in Cork, Ireland. The plan called for the navy to carry the infantry to American waters. The convoy (a fleet of ships that carries people or supplies) was supposed to meet another convoy of ships that were to sail from Boston. The Boston convoy carried more infantry commanded by Major-General Henry Clinton. The meeting was supposed to take place at the end of February off the coast of North Carolina.

Bad weather kept the ships from reaching Cork until the end of December. Then the weather kept the convoy windbound, or stuck, in Cork until February 12, 1776. Gales in the Atlantic scattered the convoy and slowed progress. The meeting between the two fleets finally came at the end of April. It was more than two months behind schedule.

Governor Martin, the royal governor of North Carolina, had hoped that the fleet would come in time to help his force of Regulators and Highlanders. Instead, two months before the fleet's arrival they had already lost the Battle of Moore's Creek. General Howe hoped to pick up some of Martin's army and use them to help capture Charleston. Instead, he had to go ahead without them.

Members of the Continental Congress first thought that Charleston might be attacked on January 1, 1776. Congress ordered South Carolina to raise more forces to defend the colony. The Americans planned to defend Charleston by building forts on the low, sandy islands just off the South Carolina coast.

The entrance to Charleston harbor was six miles from the city. The ship channel ran between Sullivan's Island on the north and James Island on the south. Back in September 1775 the rebels had captured a British fort, Fort Johnson, on James Island. In January 1776 the rebels began building a fort on Sullivan's Island. A true fort needed to be built out of stone. Instead, the Americans had to use palmetto logs. (Palmetto trees are common in South Carolina and have very strong wood.) They built parallel lines of logs 16 feet apart and filled the space with sand.

British ships arrived off Charleston on June 1, 1776. Their arrival scared the people of Charleston. They worried that the British force would sail past the forts and attack the city. Instead, the commander of the infantry, General Clinton, decided to land at an undefended place called Long Island. Clinton planned to use Long Island as a base to march against Charleston and surround the city. To do so, the infantry had to march over a channel called the Breach. Guides had told Clinton that he could cross the Breach at low tide. Instead, it turned out that the water was seven feet deep in the Breach.

Clinton saw that he had to make a new plan. He asked the commander of the British fleet, Sir Peter Parker, how he could help the fleet capture the American forts. Parker answered that his ships could defeat the forts on their own.

The Americans also had problems. Congress had sent

Because he had military experience and spoke well, many American leaders thought that Major-General Charles Lee was the most brilliant leader on the rebel side. Lee commanded all the rebel forces in the South in the spring and summer of 1776.

Major-General Charles Lee to take command of the defense of Charleston. Lee looked at the fort on Sullivan's Island. The rebels had named the fort after its commander, Colonel William Moultrie. Fort Moultrie was only half finished when the British appeared. Lee said it was a trap. The fort would become a "slaughter pen" when the British attacked. Lee wanted to retreat before an attack came. The patriot governor of South Carolina, John Rutledge, insisted that the fort be defended. Lee asked Colonel Moultrie if he could hold the fort. Moultrie answered, "Yes, I think I can."

The British fleet attacked on June 28, 1776. Inside the fort were 413 infantry and 22 gunners to serve 26 pieces of artillery. The defenders were short of gunpowder and shot for the artillery. The British fleet pounded the fort with more than 100 heavy naval guns. It seemed hopeless for the fort's garrison. Then came a lucky break. Three British ships tried to sail into a better position. They all ran aground, or got stuck

The Battle of Fort Moultrie, showing the inside of the fort with the British fleet in the distance.

Opposite: Sergeant William Jasper raises the South Carolina flag at Fort Moultrie.

in some shallow water. After several hours two of the ships got free. The third ship could not move.

Meanwhile, the American gunners fired their artillery at the stuck ships and at the *Bristol*. The *Bristol* carried 50 guns and was Parker's flagship, or headquarters ship. The Americans hit the *Bristol* 70 times. One shell struck the *Bristol* and exploded. The explosion blew the pants off Commodore Parker! More seriously, the American fire killed 64 sailors and wounded another 161 who were on the *Bristol*.

The British fire caused little damage. The spongy palmetto logs did not splinter like ordinary wood. With the sand backing, the logs absorbed the blows from the ships' cannons. At one point a British shot knocked the American flag off its flagstaff. The flag fell outside of the fort. Sergeant William Jasper bravely went outside, picked up the flag, returned, and raised it back up the flagstaff.

At sunset the British fire slowed. By 11 P.M. the fleet retreated except for the one ship still stuck. The next morning the British burned that ship to keep it from being captured by the Americans. During the battle the Americans lost about 12 killed and 17 wounded, 5 of whom later died. The British lost about 225 sailors. Three weeks later Clinton retreated from Long Island and sailed to New York City.

The Americans won the battle for two reasons: The defenders had fought bravely; the attackers had made many mistakes. The American victory was lucky. There was plenty of deep water near the place where the three British ships ran aground. If the ships had missed the shallow water, they could have fired against the side and rear of Fort Moultrie. That was the part of the fort that was not yet finished. The defenders would have had to leave the fort.

The early war battles in the South, from Great Bridge to Fort Moultrie, were important. The patriot victories discouraged the growth of the loyalist movement. They encouraged the spirit of the rebels. Most important, the victories prevented the British from conquering the southern colonies at the beginning of the war. That area stayed safely in patriot hands for the next three years, until the British returned in 1779.

The Men Who Signed the Declaration of Independence

The Declaration of Independence created the United States of America out of 13 British colonies and gave a long list of reasons for doing so. Near the top of the list was:

"We hold these truths to be self-evident, that all men are created equal, that they are endowed by their Creator with certain unalienable Rights, that among these, are Life, Liberty, and the pursuit of Happiness."

A total of 56 men signed the Declaration of Independence. A few of them had names that are still well known today: Thomas Jefferson (see below), John Hancock (see below), Benjamin Franklin, Samuel Adams (see Volume 1), and John Adams (see Volume 1). The rest were leaders in their own time, but their names are not so well known today. Most came from wealthy families. The few who did not worked to advance themselves by studying law or going into business.

All of them showed great courage by signing one piece of paper. If the colonies had not won their independence from England, these men would probably have been hanged as traitors. To protect the signers, their names were kept secret for over a year. After their names were published, the British burned the homes of fifteen of them, imprisoned one, and imprisoned the wife of another. Several had to go into hiding to avoid capture.

The signers knew that they might have to give their lives for their country. Indeed, the document ends with the words "for the support of this Declaration, . . . we mutually pledge to each other our Lives, our Fortunes, and our sacred Honour."

Here are some of their stories.

GEORGE CLYMER was born in Philadelphia in 1739. He was left an orphan and raised by a wealthy uncle. He became a successful merchant. During the Revolution's hard winter of 1776-77 Clymer bravely stayed in Philadelphia, risking capture by the British, while most of the congressmen fled to Baltimore. He and two other congressmen stayed to help run the government and get supplies for the Continental Army. Clymer lived until 1813.

JOHN HANCOCK's signature appears above all the other signatures on the Declaration of Independence. This is because he was president of the Continental Congress at the time of the signing. His signature has a fame of its own: When people are asked to sign something, they are sometimes told, "Put your 'John Hancock' on this." Hancock was born in 1737 in Massachusetts. He was orphaned and raised by a wealthy relative. He graduated from Harvard, went into business, and took an active part in revolutionary politics. Hancock expected to be named commander-in-chief of the Continental Army and was disappointed when Washington got the position. During the Revolution he commanded 6,000 militiamen in his home state. After the war he served many terms as governor of Massachusetts. He died at the age of 56.

THOMAS JEFFERSON was born in Virginia in 1743. He attended college and became a lawyer. He served in the Virginia House of Burgesses and became involved in revolutionary politics. Jefferson was a poor public speaker but an excellent writer, and his skill as a writer led to his being asked to write the Declaration of Independence. He became governor of Virginia during the Revolution. In 1800 Thomas Jefferson narrowly won election as president of the United States. He lived until 1826.

FRANCIS LEWIS was born in Wales, part of Great Britain, in 1713. He was orphaned and raised by relatives. He moved to London and went into business, and then moved to America in 1738. He started successful businesses in New York and Philadelphia, sailed around the world on a trading ship, and survived two shipwrecks. After he signed the Declaration, the British destroyed his New York home and arrested his wife. George Washington made sure that she was exchanged for a British prisoner, but being in prison ruined her health, and she died a few years later. Lewis himself lived until 1802.

ROGER SHERMAN was born in Massachusetts in 1721, the son of a cobbler, or shoemaker. He did not receive much education and went to work at his father's trade, but he read a lot in his spare time. At the age of 22 Sherman moved to Connecticut and taught himself law. He held many public offices before serving in the Continental Congress. He also signed the U.S. Constitution. He lived to the age of 72.

GEORGE WALTON, born in Virginia in 1741, was orphaned and apprenticed to a carpenter. Poor orphans often had to support themselves by being apprenticed to a trade. An apprentice worked a certain number of years in exchange for training, food, and a place to live. When Walton finished his apprenticeship, he moved to Georgia, studied law, and became a lawyer. He convinced many powerful people in Georgia to support the revolutionary cause. As a member of the Continental Congress, he remained in Philadelphia with George Clymer during the winter of 1776-77 (see above) to run the government, sharing the risk of capture. Walton was wounded during the Revolution while fighting in Georgia. He then served as the state governor and as a judge. He died in 1804.

CHAPTER SEVEN

The Declaration of Independence

The Continental Congress sent out riders to present the Declaration of Independence to each of the colonies, thereafter to be called states.

On June 7, 1776, Virginian Richard Henry Lee made a statement, or resolution, in Congress "that these United Colonies are, and of right ought to be, free and independent States." John Adams of Massachusetts seconded the motion. Many patriots disagreed. They still hoped that if only Great Britain agreed to some important changes, America could stay as part of the British empire.

Still, four days later Congress elected Thomas Jefferson, John Adams, Benjamin Franklin, Roger Sherman, and Robert R. Livingston to write a declaration about independence. All of them worked on the project. Thomas Jefferson, then 33 years old, is considered the major author.

The Declaration of Independence is the most famous American political document in U.S. history. It clearly and powerfully explained why the colonies were in revolt against King George. On July 4 Congress voted to accept the declaration. During the night of July 4-5 copies were printed for the army and the states. The next day riders carried the copies to the army and to the state legislatures. The legend exists that the Declaration of Independence was signed on July 4, 1776. That is not true. In fact, the official copy was not signed until August 2, 1776, and several signatures were added after that date.

The Declaration of Independence created a new nation, the United States of America. It changed the American rebellion from an effort to secure rights within the British empire to a struggle to become completely free of British control. No one had thought that the Boston Tea Party, Lexington and Concord, and Bunker Hill would lead to this.

The newly born United States faced many problems in its war for independence. Before, America had traded its farm goods for British manufactured goods and products such as sugar from the West Indies. The war ended all such trade. America produced very few military supplies such as guns and gunpowder. The Continental Army would have only two sources of manufactured supplies: things it captured from the British and supplies that passed through the British

The signing of the Declaration of Independence.

naval blockade. For that reason the army would always be short of essential military supplies such as uniforms, tents, and blankets.

It was very difficult to move from one part of the country to another. Trade and commerce, the exchange of goods, including food, normally moved along the rivers to the Atlantic Ocean. Since the British controlled the ocean, goods had to move by land. But there were not very many roads running north and south. There were not enough wagons, nor horses to haul the wagons. That meant that while one area might grow enough food to feed the army, there was no way to move the food to the army. The Continental Army was almost always hungry, especially during the winter.

The thirteen states had a total population of about 2.5 million people. About one in five males were black slaves. Because of the attitudes of the time most blacks were not eligible for military service. About one-third of white males were loyal to the British government. Most

Most American men of military age were farmers. They hung their hunting weapons over the fireplace in their homes. They needed to stay home to feed and protect their families. To leave home to fight in the war was a difficult decision.

of the remaining males of military age were farmers who had married at a young age and immediately started families. Their first loyalty was to their families, their second to their farms, because unless they worked their farms, their families would starve. Even if such men agreed with the ideas of the Revolution, they were not likely to join the Continental Army. Joining the army meant enlisting for long periods of time, and these men could not afford to do it. They greatly preferred to serve for a short amount of time in the militia.

The newly born United States was a grouping, or confederation, of thirteen independent states. These states had little or no history of working together as a nation. They were like children: each determined to do whatever they wanted, united only in their desire to defeat their parent, Great Britain.

To fight a war efficiently requires a strong government, or central authority. Such an authority can gather resources—money, men, weapons, supplies—for a long struggle. A central authority can persuade individual people and individual states to sacrifice for the good of the whole nation. During the Revolutionary War the United States did not have a working central authority.

Wars are very expensive. Yet the Continental Congress did not have a way to pay for the war. The power to tax

During the Revolutionary War paper money, like this twenty-dollar bill, was something new.

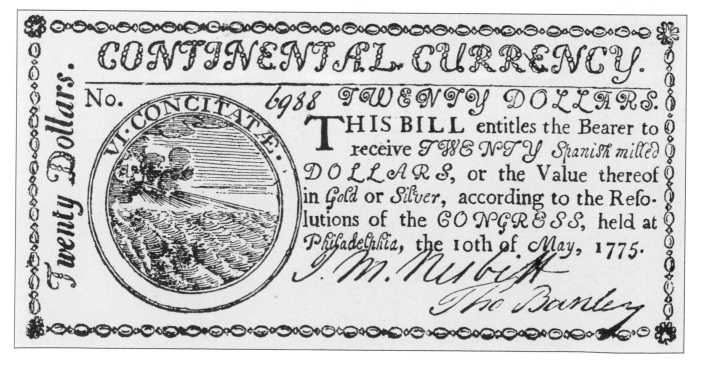

was in the hands of the states. Congress could and did ask the states for money. Sometimes the states agreed; more often they could not or did not. So, the Continental Congress printed paper money. At first people accepted the paper money. The war could not have continued without paper money. But Congress, and then the states, kept printing more and more paper money. As time passed, the paper money became less and less valuable. The expression "not worth a Continental dollar" entered the American language. So, the Continental soldiers went for long periods without pay. Equally bad, the special officers who were supposed to get food and supplies for the army did not have money to buy those things.

Here then were the major trends, or themes, that made a difference for the entire war. First, the rebel leaders would find it very hard to gather and keep an army. Instead, there would be a small group of professional soldiers, the Continental Army, and a much bigger group of civilian-soldiers, namely, the militia. Second, there would be a constant battle between the patriot leaders who saw the need for a strong central authority to run the war and the patriot leaders who strongly disagreed.

Because of that conflict the army would almost always be poorly supplied. Often the soldiers were near starvation. George Washington, and all patriots, had to find a way somehow to win the war in spite of these problems.

The fight for independence depended upon American Continental soldiers like these Delaware soldiers who are leaving Dover, Delaware to join Washington's army.

Chronology

June 14, 1775: The Second Continental Congress votes to enlist soldiers directly into Continental service.

June 15, 1775: George Washington is appointed general and commander-in-chief of the Continental Army.

June 17, 1775: The British win the Battle of Bunker Hill by capturing ground and driving off the rebels, but many more British than rebels are killed or wounded.

July 2, 1775: General Washington arrives at Cambridge, Massachusetts, to take command of the Continental Army.

November 2, 1775: Patriot General Richard Montgomery and his troops capture St. Johns in Canada.

December 1775: England orders large numbers of British army troops to sail to America.

December 9, 1775: Patriots win at the Battle of Great Bridge, Virginia, the first battle between patriots and the British since Bunker Hill.

December 31, 1775: Patriot troops make a disastrous attack against Quebec.

January 1, 1776: The royal governor of Virginia orders the bombardment of Norfolk and destroys the city, causing most Virginia colonists to turn against the British.

January 25, 1776: Colonel Henry Knox arrives at Boston with artillery after a long winter trek from Fort Ticonderoga.

February 27, 1776: Patriot forces win the Battle of Moore's Creek, North Carolina.

March 17, 1776: British troops evacuate Boston.

June 1, 1776: British ships carrying army troops finally arrive off Charleston, South Carolina, several months behind schedule.

June 28, 1776: British ships attack Fort Moultrie, outside Charleston, South Carolina, but cannot defeat the Americans.

July 4, 1776: The Second Continental Congress votes to accept the Declaration of Independence. This is the first time that the colonies clearly state that they will fight to be an independent nation.

Glossary

ARTILLERY: a group of cannons and other large guns used to help an army by firing at enemy troops

BATTERY: a group of four to six large guns that makes up the basic artillery unit. A battery also includes the soldiers trained to fire the guns and the horses or mules that move the guns.

BRIGADE: an army unit usually made up of four or more regiments. Three or more brigades usually make up a division.

CABINET: a group of government officials that advises and reports to the head of a nation, such as the British prime minister or the American president

CAMPAIGN: a series of military actions that are connected because they have the same goal

CAVALRY: a group of soldiers that moves and fights on horseback

COMMANDER-IN-CHIEF: the person having the highest authority over a military force

COMPANY: a small army unit numbering 25 to 50 men. Eight or ten companies make up a regiment.

CONTINENTAL: referring to the thirteen united colonies in America. Continental soldiers served in the regular American army.

DEFENSES: a line of fieldworks and forts around an area that an army is defending

DIVISION: a large army unit usually made up of three or more brigades

INFANTRY: soldiers who fight on foot, or foot soldiers

LOYALIST: an American colonist who wanted America to remain part of the British empire; also called a Tory

MILITIA: a group of citizens not normally part of the army that mobilizes for the purpose of defending their homeland in an emergency; also used as a plural to describe several such groups

MUSKET: a smoothbore, single-shot gun used by infantry in battle. Muskets were not as accurate as rifles.

PATRIOT: an American who wanted the colonies to be independent of the British empire; from patriotic, which means devoted to the good of one's country; also called rebel

REGIMENT: an army unit made up of eight or ten companies. A regiment at full strength had about 450 soldiers.

REGULARS: professional soldiers who belong to the army full time

SABER: a heavy, curved sword carried by cavalrymen. The curve makes it easier for them to strike downward while on horseback.

SECRETARY OF STATE: a national government official in charge of all dealings with other nations

SIEGE: a campaign to capture a place by surrounding it, cutting it off from supplies, and attacking it cautiously by advancing under the cover of trenches and earthworks

SKIRMISH: a brief battle involving a small number of soldiers; often part of a larger battle

STAFF: soldiers assigned to help officers make and carry out the plans

STRATEGY: the overall plan for organizing troops to fight a battle or campaign

Further Resources

Books:

Adams, Russell B., Jr., ed. *The Revolutionaries*. Alexandria, VA: Time-Life Books, 1996.

Brenner, Barbara. *If You Were There in 1776.* New York: Bradbury Press, 1994. Details of daily life in the rebellious colonies in 1776.

Dolan, Edward F. *The American Revolution: How We Fought the War of Independence.* Brookfield, CT: Millbrook Press, 1995.

Fleming, Thomas. *First in Their Hearts: A Biography of George Washington.* Lakeville, CT: Grey Castle Press, 1984.

Martin, J. P. Private Yankee Doodle. Fort Washington, PA: Eastern Acorn Press, 1998. The entire diary of Joseph Plumb Martin, who enlisted in the Continental army when he was 15.

Moscow, Henry. *Thomas Jefferson and His World.* New York: American Heritage Publishing Co., 1960.

Murphy, Jim. *A Young Patriot: The American Revolution as Experienced by One Boy.* New York: Clarion Books, 1996. Based on the life story of a real person, Joseph Plumb Martin, who was 15 years old when he enlisted in the Continental Army.

Peacock, Louise. *Crossing The Delaware: A History in Many Voices.* New York: Atheneum, 1998.

Quinn, Brother C. Edwin. *The Signers of the Declaration of Independence.* New York: Bronx County Historical Society, 1988.

Wilbur, C. Keith. *The Revolutionary Soldier, 1775–1783.* Old Saybrook, CT: Globe Pequot Press, 1993.

Websites:

http://library.thinkquest.org/10966/
The Revolutionary War—A Journey Towards Freedom

http://ushistory.org/march/index.html
Virtual Marching Tour of the American Revolution

http://www.pbs.org/ktca/liberty/game/index.html
The Road to Revolution—A Revolutionary Game

http://www.pbs.org/ktca/liberty/chronicle/index.html
Chronicle of the Revolution
Read virtual newspapers of the Revolutionary era

http://www.vboston.com/VBoston/Content/FreedomTrail/Index.cfm

Places to Visit:

Independence National Historical Park, Philadelphia, Pennsylvania
        The place where the Continental Congress met.

Monticello, Charlottesville, Virginia
        Thomas Jefferson's home, full of his many inventions.

About the Authors

James R. Arnold has written more than 20 books on military history topics and contributed to many others. Roberta Wiener has coauthored several books with Mr. Arnold and edited numerous educational books, including a children's encyclopedia. They live and farm in Virginia.

Set Index

Bold numbers refer to volumes; *italics* refer to illustrations

60–63; **2:** 11, 44, 52; **3:** 6, 9; **4:** 12, 29, 63;
5: 6–7, 14, 25; **7:** 62, 68; **8:** 32, 61; **9:** 57;
10: 22–23, 49, *67*

Georgia **1:** 12, 58, 60; **7:** 43, 65–68; **8:** 27–29,
36, 55–56, 61, 65; **9:** 16, 30, 44, 58, 63;
10: 45, 61
    Savannah **1:** 12; **7:** 65–66; **8:** 27, 29–31, 48,
56, 61; **9:** 6, 68; **10:** 25

Germain, George **3:** *6–8,* 37; **4:** 10, 14; **5:** 6–8,
11, 14; **7:** 41; **8:** 48; **9:** 31; **10:** 22

German Battalion **4:** 52, 58

Germantown (Pa.), battle **6:** 36–41, 63

Girty, Simon **8:** 11, 16

Glover, John **4:** 28, 38, 53, 66

Government, United States **10:** 38–40
    Political parties **10:** 39, 42

de Grasse, Francois **8:** *29;* **10:** 10, 13, *15,* 25

Graves, Thomas **10:** 13, 15, 21

Great Bridge (Va.), battle **3:** 49

Great Britain; see British; also see England

Green Mountain Boys **2:** 50–51; **3:** 28; **5:** 24

Greene, Christopher **7:** 36

Greene, Nathanael **2:** 54; **4:** 24, 31–32, 43;
6: 20–21, *24,* 28, 52; **7:** 50, 55.59; **8:** 47, 55;
9: 25–32, 44, 46–47, 49–52, 55–60, 62–65,
67–68; **10:** 9, 12, 25, 57, *61*

Grey, Charles **6:** 31–32

Grierson, Benjamin **9:** 63

Guerillas; see also Partisans **4:** 8; **8:** 62; **9:** 16,
29, 35

Guilford Courthouse (N.C.), battle **9:** 49–58,
62; **10:** 12, 57

Hale, Nathan **4:** 40; **9:** 15

Hamilton, Alexander **4:** 56, 61, 66; **6:** 53;
8: 59; **10:** 18, *39,* 45, *62*

Hamilton, Henry **8:** 9, 14–15

Hancock, John **2:** 6–7, 19, 24–25, 46; **3:** 60

Hand, Edward **4:** 58, 66; **8:** 23

Harlem Heights (N.Y.), battle **4:** 32, *34–35, 36,*
38

Hart, Nancy **8:** 64

Hausegger, Nicholas **4:** 52, 58

Heath, William **4:** 42; **10:** 13

Henry, Patrick **1:** *38–39,* 40, 44, 59; **3:** 11,
46–48; **8:** 11, 14; **10:** 39, *62*

Herkimer, Nicholas **5:** 41–*42*

Hessians **4:** 12–15, 48–49, 52, 53, 55–57, 63;

5: *11,* 14, 20, 23, 25, 29, *33–35,* 61; **6:** 24,
26, 30, 41–42, 58; **7:** 37, 40, 48, 52; **8:** 46;
10: 57

Hobkirk's Hill (S.C.), battle **9:** 59–60, 62

Hopkins, Esek **7:** *13,* 15–16

Horses; see also Cavalry **3:** *20,* 22; **4:** 9–10;
5: 29, 58; **6:** 19; **8:** 49, 53

Howard, John **9:** 34, 39, 42

Howe, Richard **4:** 21, 29–*30;* **6:** 19; **7:** 35, 40,
43, 58–60; **10:** *67*

Howe, Robert **7:** 65–66

Howe, William **2:** 55, 60–61, 63; **3:** 10–11, 37,
42, 44; **4:** 6, 11, 14, 21–22, 25, 27, 29, 36,
38–40, 42–43, 62–63, 66; **5:** 6–7, 9–11, 26,
56; **6:** 9–13, 16–19, 22, 25, 28–31, 33, 35–36,
41, 56–57, 60; **10:** *67*

Hubbardton (N.Y.), battle **5:** 24–25, 32

Huddy, Joshua **10:** 24

Hudson Highlands **4:** 42; **5:** 11, 48, 55–57;
6: 8; **8:** 37; **9:** 11–12, 14

Hudson River **4:** 21–24, 40, 42–43, 52, 63;
5: 7, 10–11, 16, 27–29, 40, 45–48, 51, 55,
57–59; **6:** 8, 12, 16; **8:** 37, 39; **9:** 11; **10:** 10

Huger, Isaac **9:** 59–60

Hutchinson, Thomas **1:** 40

Illinois
    Kaskaskia **8:** 13

Indians; see Native Americans

Indiana
    Vincennes **8:** 13–15

Ireland **3:** 54; **4:** 12; **7:** 33

Iroquois; see also Native Americans **5:** 17;
8: 16–18, 23, 25–26; **10:** 49–50

Jasper, William **3:** *58–59;* **8:** 31

Jay, John **4:** 32; **10:** 31, 39, *44–45*

Jefferson, Thomas **1:** 44; **2:** 46; **3:** 61–62; **9:** 27;
10: 34–35

Johnson, Guy **8:** 18

Johnson, William **8:** 18

Jones, David **5:** 32

Jones, John Paul **7:** *20–22,* 24, 26–27, 30–32;
10: *41*

de Kalb **6:** *20–21;* **8:** *55,* 59–*60*

Kaskaskia (Ill.) **8:** 13

Kettle Creek (Ga.), battle **7:** 67–68

Acknowledgments

Author's collection: 38
Anne S. K. Brown Military Collection, John Hay Library, Brown University, Providence, Rhode Island: 19, 20, 34, 41, 44–45
Colonial Williamsburg Foundation: 63
Rudolf Cronau, *The Army of the American Revolution and its Organizer*, 1923: 14, 22–23
Fort Ticonderoga Museum: 39
Guilford Courthouse National Military Park: 21B
Independence National Historical Park: 26T, 35T, 37, 46, 49T
Library of Congress:, 6–7, 11, 12, 30, 31, 32, 33, 35, 48, 49B, 54, 61, 62, 66
Massachusetts Historical Society: 10
Military Archive & Research Services, England: 65
Moores Creek National Battlefield: 50, 51
National Archives: 15, 17, 26, 55, 64
National Archives of Canada: 29
National Park Service: 42–43 *Preparation for Battle*, copyright Louis S. Glanzman, 52
The George C. Neumann Collection, a gift of the Sun Company to Valley Forge National Historical Park, 1978: 18B, 21T
U.S. Marine Corps, Washington D.C.: 13 *The First Recruits December 1775*, by Charles Waterhouse, 1974
U.S. Naval Academy Museum, courtesy Beverly R. Robinson Collection: 24–25
U.S. Naval Historical Center, Washington, D.C.: Front cover, 46–47,
U.S. Government Printing Office: 8, 9, 28, 58
U.S. Senate Collection: 56–57
West Point Museum Collection, United States Military Academy: 18T photograph by Anthony Mairo, Gateway Studio, Fishkill, NY

Maps by Jerry Malone